*Stories on the bonus CD are from the Wild & Wacky Totally True Bible Stories audio series and are not in read-along format with this book.

"Smarter Than God?"
Adam & Eve (6:10)
from the full-length CD:
All about OBEDIENCE

"Wilderness Wanderers"
Moses (8:46)
from the full-length CD:
All about OBEDIENCE

"Boat Buildin'"
Noah (8:13)
from the full-length CD:
All about FAITH

"Renegade Soldier"
David & Goliath (7:38)
from the full-length CD:
All about COURAGE

"The Prodigal Son"
Jesus' Parable (6:49)
from the full-length CD:
All about FORGIVENESS

"Jesus' Birthday Party"
Visitors (5:55)
from the full-length CD:
All about CHRISTMAS

"Lazarus, Come Out"
Lazarus (7:49)
from the full-length CD:
All about MIRACLES

**"Rub-a-Dub-Dub,
Ten Toes in a Tub"**
Jesus Washes
the Disciples' Feet (6:58)
from the full-length CD:
All about HELPING OTHERS

"Spreadin' the Good News" (7:25)
from the full-length CD:
All about SALVATION

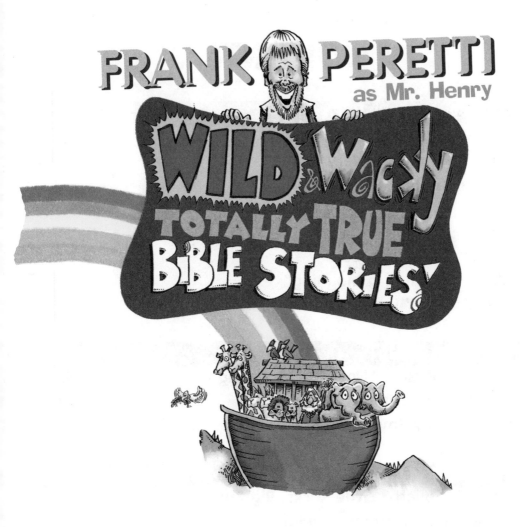

FRANK PERETTI
as Mr. Henry

WILD & Wacky TOTALLY TRUE BIBLE STORIES

With Sharon Lamson and Cheryl McKay

Illustrated by Bill Ross

www.tommynelson.com

A Division of Thomas Nelson, Inc.
www.ThomasNelson.com

CONTENTS

*Indicates NOT on audio collection

Library of Congress Cataloging-in-Publications Data

Peretti, Frank E.
  Wild & wacky totally true Bible stories / Frank Peretti, as Mr. Henry ; with Sharon Lamson, Cheryl McKay ;
illustrated by Bill Ross.
    p. cm.
    Summary: Humorous retellings of twenty-seven stories from the Old and New Testaments, grouped by such themes
as jealousy, forgiveness, courage, and obedience, with advice on applying the lessons to everyday life.
    ISBN 1-4003-0012-6
    1. Bible stories, English. [1. Bible stories. 2. Conduct of life.] I. Title: Wild and wacky totally true Bible stories.
II. Lamson, Sharon, 1948–   III. McKay, Cheryl. IV. Ross, Bill, 1956–   ill. V. Title.
BS551.3 .P47 2002
220.9'505—dc21   2002141415

Printed in America
03 04 05 06 07 QWK 9 8 7 6 5 4 3 2

6 PLAY BY THE RULES

Hi, there! I'm Mr. Henry, collector of Bible stuff and storyteller extraordinaire! Look what I've found under my couch. Here's my "Stop" sign and my "Do Not Litter" sign. But this is what I've been searching for: the **"Do Not Eat From This Tree!"** sign.

These other signs represent rules that either help protect where we live and play or keep us safe. But the "Do Not Eat from This Tree!" rule came straight from God. Let's find out if Adam and Eve obeyed His rule.

Trees with all sorts of fruit grew in the Garden—red fruit, green fruit, yummy, sweet, and juicy fruit. In the middle of the Garden, next to the tree of life, stood the tree of the knowledge of good and evil. We'll call it the **"gOOD-aND-eviL trEE."**

God told Adam, "You may eat the fruit from any tree in the garden. But you must not eat the fruit from the tree which gives the knowledge of good and evil. If you ever eat fruit from that tree, you will die!" (Genesis 2:16–17)

Adam and Eve understood the rules. They decided to explore the Garden and name all the trees.

Eve said, "Oh Adam! Come and look at this yellow fruit! I'm just **bananas** about this tree."

"Nice," said Adam. "I found some fruit too! But it's not quite red and not quite yellow."

"How colorful!" Eve answered. "What will you call it?"

"I don't know, Eve," Adam replied. "It's just so, so **orange!**"

One day, as Eve was strolling through the orchard, she heard an interesting sound.

"What is that *psssst* sound?" Eve asked aloud. "It sounds like one of the rubber trees has sprung a leak!"

"Hey! Eve! I'm over here!" hissed a big, beautiful snake. He hung down from the good-and-evil tree. Eve could see his tail pointing to one of the good-and-evil fruits.

"Eve," the snake hissed again, "I've heard through the grapevine . . ."

"Grapevine!" Eve interrupted. "I love **grapes!** Did you know that if you let grapes dry in the sun, they become raisins?"

"How interesting!" the snake replied. "But as I was saying, I've heard that God won't let you eat from the trees in the Garden. Is that true?"

Eve replied, "God said we could try fruit from any tree except the good-and-evil tree. If we even touch it, we will die!"

"Baloney!" the snake sneered. "You won't die if you taste the fruit from that tree. If you eat it, you'll be like God and know good and evil. God just doesn't want you to be as smart as He is, that's all."

"Really?" Eve asked. "Well, that fruit does look yummy."

"Tasssste it," hissed the snake. "It will make you so smart!"

CHOMP!

Eve bit into the delicious fruit.

"Oh Adam!" Eve called. "Have I got a surprise for you!"

"What is it?" Adam asked. Then he saw the bite marks on the fruit from the good-and-evil tree.

"Oh no!" he cried. "What have you done?"

"The snake said this would make me smart, and he was right," Eve said. "I feel smarter already. Come on, take a bite!"

"Well, I don't know . . ." Adam said.

"Oh, come on, Adam. Do you want me to be smarter than you?"

Adam thought for a minute, and then he took the fruit from Eve. **CHOMP! CHOMP!** He finished the whole thing!

God wasn't happy. Adam and Eve had broken God's rule, and this was a sin. Because they had disobeyed, He made them leave the Garden. And He sent weeds and thorns and pesky mosquitoes to bother them.

As for that sneaky snake who lied to them, God punished him by making him slither in the dirt on his belly the rest of his days. Ha! Eat dust, you bad snake!

That snake was wrong! Breaking God's rules is never smart. Disobeying God is sin—and sin only brings us pain and trouble. The Bible says in 1 John 5:3 that if we love God, we will obey Him. And the cool thing is, He promises that His **RuLes** will never be too hard for us to follow.

Hmmm, I wish my own rules weren't so hard to obey!

Jonah

6 SOMETHING VERY FISHY

Um, excuse me, but do you think you could come back later? I should have Bubbles's bowl clean by then. I mean, I think I will be done by then. You can barely see him because his bowl has gotten so disgusting! And it's all my fault!

This fish manual says to clean his bowl weekly, but I don't like that job. It's *slimy* and fishy smelling. I should've obeyed the manual, though. It says, "A scrub in time saves slime."

How can such a tiny fish make such an enormous stink? He smells as big as the fish that swallowed Jonah!

Jonah lived back in Bible times, when the Ninevites, a bunch of bullies, started all sorts of trouble. They never said "please" or "thank you." They cut into lines and made noise late at night. And they picked on Jewish people, who were called Israelites.

Jonah was a **PROPHET**—a deliverer of God's messages. And one day God told Jonah, "The people of Nineveh are wicked. Tell them they must turn from their wicked ways and be good, or I will punish them."

Well, Jonah couldn't stand the Ninevites because of all the bad stuff they did. He wanted God to punish them. So instead of going to Nineveh to warn them, Jonah got on a ship heading **awaaay** from Nineveh! Jonah smiled as he boarded; then he slipped below deck to take a nap.

When the ship reached the middle of the sea, a terrible storm came. The captain and sailors shook in their sandals. Then the captain commanded everyone to pray.

"Hey! Where's Jonah?" he roared.

"Here he is," yelled the first mate, "snoring in the cargo bay." They tugged and poked at Jonah until he woke up.

"There's a terrible storm!" the captain shouted. "I need everyone—including you—to pray for our safety."

"But sir," Jonah began, "I'm running away from God. If I pray now, He'll know where to find me."

KA-**BOOM!** Thunder roared as lightning flashed, and the waves rose rough around them.

"Oh no!" Jonah cried. "God must know where I am. Boy, am I in big trouble—I disobeyed God. Captain, this is all my fault. Save yourselves by throwing me overboard."

The captain and the sailors didn't like Jonah's plan. Instead, they tried to row back to shore, but the winds were too strong.

"It's no use!" the captain moaned. "Sorry, Jonah, but it's **heave-ho,** and into the sea you go!"

As soon as Jonah splashed into the sea, the sun began to shine and the winds stopped blowing.

Jonah bobbed in the water. Once. Twice. The third time he sank. Just when he thought things couldn't get worse, Jonah saw a giant mouth full of teeth coming straight at him.

Oh, great! Jonah thought. *I'm gonna be fish food!*

GULP! Jonah slid past those teeth, through a pair of giant tonsils, and down into the belly of the monster fish.

Burrrppppp!

For three days, Jonah traveled in that fishy submarine. He thought about how he'd disobeyed God. Sad and alone, Jonah realized he'd made a terrible **MiSTaKe.** He had run away from his responsibility. So he decided to pray.

"Dear Lord," he said. "I'm sorry I disobeyed You. Please forgive me. I still don't like the Ninevites, but *You* clearly do. If You get me out of this fish, I will go to Nineveh and deliver Your message."

Just then, **BELCH!** The monster fish spat Jonah right onto the beach. Jonah scraped a piece of seaweed off his forehead.

"People of Nineveh!" he shouted. "God sent me here to tell you that He's tired of your wickedness. He says that in forty days He will destroy the city, but if you turn from your wicked ways and be good, God will let you live."

The people gasped! They believed Jonah and worked to change how they acted. They quit being bullies. They learned to be polite. And most of all, they quit picking on the Israelites.

And I did what the fish manual says. Look! Bubbles's bowl is clean! Now you can watch him swim.

Doing the **right** thing isn't always easy, but obedience teaches us responsibility. If we faithfully obey when it comes to the small stuff—like cleaning the fishbowl or picking up our dirty clothes and putting them in the hamper—God promises in Matthew 25:21 that He will let us "care for much greater things."

I just hope it's not a bigger fishbowl!

6 GO BLOW YOUR HORN

Tooooooooot!

Some people around these parts call me the Rootin'-Tootin' Lumberjack. "Mr. Henry the Rootin'-Tootin' Lumberjack," they say. And I say, "Yup, that's me." I've been knocking down trees since I was knee-high to a sapling, I have. Well . . . I did trim the hedges all by myself once.

But this poor tree is dead. It has to go, or it could fall on my house. I figure if I march around long enough blowing my horn, it'll fall—just as the walls of Jericho fell for Joshua.

Joshua had to conquer Jericho to reach the Promised Land. So he sent two spies into the city to check things out.

They met a woman named Rahab who lived in the city's wall. Rahab hid the spies because they were God's men. But she made them promise to spare her and her family when the Israelites conquered Jericho.

The spies promised, saying, "Tie a **red rope** in your window, and make sure your family is safe at home when we charge the city."

Long after the spies had returned to camp, Joshua awoke. When he stuck his head out of his tent, a tall ANGEL carrying a big sword appeared right in front of him.

"I have come as the commander of the Lord's army!" the angel declared.

Joshua bowed down. "Your command is my wish . . . I mean, um, your wish is my command," he stammered.

"Take off your sandals," ordered the angel. "You are on holy ground."

Then the Lord told Joshua how to conquer Jericho. But His plan was, well, a bit unusual.

"March around the city with your army one time every day for six days," the Lord said. "Have seven priests carry trumpets made from rams' horns. Then, on the seventh day, march around the city seven times and have the priests blow the trumpets as they walk. Blow one long blast on the trumpets, and have all your people shout! The walls of Jericho will FALL DOWN, and you can destroy the city."

Joshua obeyed God. Joshua instructed the Israelites, "March around the city once and come back to camp."

The soldiers stationed atop Jericho's walls saw Israel's army approach.

"Uh-oh," said the first soldier. "Looks like we have company."

The other soldier yelled out, "**Yoo-hoo!** Israelite army! Are you playing Ring-around-the-City?"

The rude soldiers snickered and snorted, but the Israelites continued to march.

They marched again on the second day. Jericho's soldiers chuckled even more.

"Losers!" they jeered. "Hey, Lame-o! Do you need a map so you can find your way home?"

Every day the Israelites marched and were mocked. But on the sixth day, Jericho's soldiers started to chew their fingernails.

"You know what? They're making me **nervous**," said one.

"Me too," agreed the other. "Whatever they're up to, I don't like it."

Finally day seven dawned. The priests carried their horns, tromped around Jericho, and trumpeted as loudly as they could. Seven times they marched around Jericho. Finally, the priests gave a long, loud blast on their horns, and all the Israelites shouted. What a ruckus!

The walls of Jericho crumbled beneath the nasty soldiers' feet, and Israel's army charged into the city. Just as God had promised, Jericho lay in ruin.

As for Rahab and her family, they invited Joshua and the spies to celebrate with yards and yards of red rope **licorice** and tiny squares of Jericho crumb cake!

That plan worked because it was *God's* plan, and Joshua obeyed it. Maybe that's why my blowing a horn and stomping around this tree hasn't made it fall. It was my plan, not God's.

In Jeremiah 29:11, God says, "I know what I have planned for you. . . . I plan to give you hope and a good future." God definitely knows what's best.

And it seems the best way to do this job is to use a little muscle!

Timber!

6 A WAY BIG BOAT

Whack!

I bonk my head on that board all the time. When we built this workshop, my builder said to never, ever remove this piece of wood, or the whole roof would cave in! But it sure hurts when I smack my head on this thing.

It should say, "Watch out!"

Instead it says, **"NOAH's BIG BOAT."**

Let me tell you the story of Noah and his boat . . .

There once lived a man named Noah, one of the most faithful guys in the whole Bible. One bright day, as Noah watered his garden, he heard a voice calling, "Noooaaahhhh! Noah!"

"Is that You, God?" Noah asked.

"Yes. I must tell you that I plan to destroy the earth and every living creature. I am sad that I ever made all these things. The people are mean and **wicked** except for you and your family. So I will make it rain until the whole earth floods. To save your family, you will need a really big boat."

God told Noah how big to build his boat—450 feet long, 75 feet wide, and 45 feet high. Way **BIG!** Noah's neighbors watched, amused, as he worked in his front yard.

Like all the other people, these neighbors were not nice at all. That's why God planned to give the whole world a good, cleansing bath. Even though his neighbors made fun of him, Noah's faith in God gave him the strength to obey.

"Noah's gone nutso," one neighbor scoffed.

"Yep. He's bonkers," said another.

God sent two of every animal—one female and one male—to Noah's boat. "Step right up," Noah yelled to the zebras. "Don't be shy," he called to the tigers.

Noah welcomed the dogs, cats, alligators, gerbils, koala bears, and all the other animals. Then Noah gathered his family.

"Everyone, it's time to go on our family cruise."

"With all these animals?" Noah's son Ham whined. "I'm allergic to zebras."

"**Achoo!** And to monkeys," added Ham's wife.

Just then, raindrops started to fall. Forgetting all about their allergies, Noah's family leaped into the boat.

The rain **POUNDED** down as Noah's neighbors begged him to take them, too.

"Noah! We want to go with you!"

But Noah couldn't let them in. God had sealed the door.

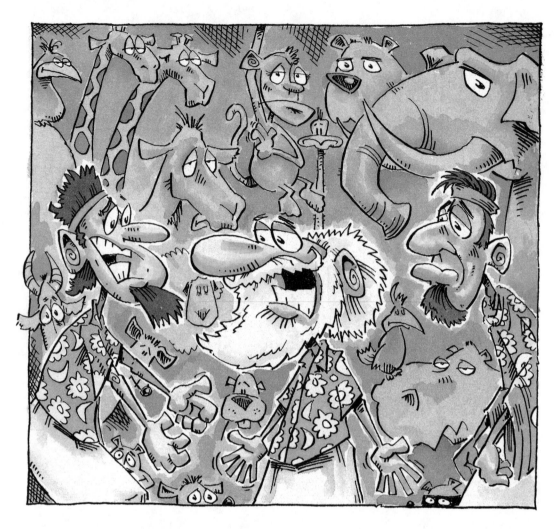

Just as God had declared, it poured for forty long days and even longer nights. They seemed especially long for Noah and his family, who felt like chickens cooped up with the chickens.

"Hey, Papa! I thought you said this family vacation would be like a cruise," moaned Noah's son Japheth.

"Yeah!" chimed in Noah's other son, Shem. "What happened to five-course meals? I'm sharing a stateroom with a giraffe."

"Boys!" Noah yelled. "Stop your whining. Our faithful God is taking good care of us. Ever heard of being thankful?"

Finally the rain stopped. But water still covered the earth for a long time.

Then one day, Noah sent a dove to search for land. When the dove flew back carrying an **olive** leaf, Noah knew the bird had found a dry patch. Two months later, God told Noah that everyone could get out of the boat.

Noah's family ran around on the bright-green grass, playing tag. As he watched the animals chase each other, Noah heard a voice.

"Noooaaahhhh! Noah!"

"Yes, God," he answered, as a moose licked his nose.

"I promise that I will never again send a flood to destroy the earth."

Noah smiled, and God sealed His promise with a RAINBOW

God always does what He says He will. God promised Noah He would take care of his family. Sure enough, God delivered.

Do you have enough **faith** to obey God, even if He asks you to do something that sounds weird? Even if people make fun of you? Being faithful worked for Noah! It can work for you, too!

WHINING & MOANING

It seems like there's always something to clean up around here. I hate cleaning. First I have to put everything away, and then I have to wipe down, dust off, and sweep away the dirt.

Now, *who* left this old box of Manna Wafers on the mantel? Wow. Listen to me. I'm complaining just like a bunch of **"moan-heads"** did way back in Moses' time. If they had just obeyed God without bellyaching, their lives might have been a lot easier.

One day, when Moses and the Israelites were backpacking to the Promised Land, God told Moses to meet Him on top of Mount Sinai. He wanted to give Moses some instructions He'd written on two **STONE** tablets.

Before Moses left, he gathered everyone together. "Okay, listen up," he said. "I'm going to be tied up in an important meeting with God. While I'm gone, I'm leaving Aaron in charge!"

Imagine! A meeting with God. The people thought that was pretty cool—at least, for a while.

But soon they began to complain. "When's Moses coming back?" they whined to Aaron. "He's been gone forever! Make us some nice shiny gods so we can worship them and have fun! Pleeease!"

Aaron *should* have said, "Are you nuts? No way!" But he didn't.

Instead, Aaron said, "Okay, travelers, wanderers, and tagalongs, lend me your earrings!"

They melted the earrings and made a golden calf. Then came PARTY time . . .

Meanwhile, God told Moses what was happening below. Moses stormed down that mountainside. When he saw the golden calf, he practically had a cow. "You want to party?!" he yelled. "We're going to make a pot of Golden Calf Soup— and you're going to eat every drop!"

Then Moses made the people start their journey again. And even though they'd been bad, God provided them with good food. They called it **"MANNA."** But the people got tired of manna.

Soon *everyone* began to yell: "Meat! Meat! We want meat!"
God grew very angry, and Moses got upset too.

"Lord," Moses cried, "why am I in charge of these moan-heads? I'm not their daddy or their nanny. Where am I supposed to get meat for all these people?"

Well, God came through again. He gave the people meat. In fact, He gave them a lot of meat! So much that the people actually got sick of it—and sick to their stomachs. Did they learn a lesson from this? Nope!

Even though God met their needs, the people started to **complain** *again*.

One girl said, "I hate marching in the desert. Sand gets all in my shoes."

Someone else cried, "Sand and manna. Manna and sand. We've got no bread. No water. No air conditioners!"

Then a little boy yelled out, pointing, "Hey! What are those?"

"SNAKES!"

Hundreds of snakes slithered toward them. Snakes glided through the campsite and wriggled into tents. Some began to bite people. Lots of people got sick, and many of them died.

"Please, Moses," others begged. "Ask God to get rid of these snakes! They scare us!"

So Moses prayed, but God didn't send away the snakes. Instead, He told Moses to make a bronze snake and put it on a pole.

"Okay, people," Moses said. "I'm going to put this snake where everyone can see it. If you get bitten, just look at the bronze snake, and you won't die."

Do you think that put an end to all the complaining? Well, can snakes fly? Ha!

The moan-heads hadn't obeyed God in the beginning, and they didn't obey Him later, either. They could have reached the Promised Land in just a few weeks, but because of their disobedience, it took them **forty** years!

If we have faith in God, we will do what He asks of us. I think I'll finish my cleaning without being a moan-head, and I can start by "polishing off" this box of Manna Wafers.

Daniel

6 LIONS' LUNCHMEAT

It must be here somewhere. If only I could find it . . . It's not in the breadbox. It's not under the table. Ah yes! Now I remember! It's in the oven. I'm sure of it.

I must have left it there when I baked rock cookies. Or was that the day I made rock candy? Never mind, here it is—the rock that kept Daniel from escaping a scary lions' den.

But Daniel knew that God would take care of him. When Daniel was **tRappEd** in that lions' den, God saved him! Let me tell you the story.

There once lived a king with a really looong name: Nebuchadnezzar. Let's just call him King Nebbie. He felt crabbier than a crab cake because he had so many **bad** dreams. But a wise man named Daniel came to help him.

King Nebbie asked, "Can you tell me what my dreams mean?"

Daniel answered, "I can't, but God can."

The king told Daniel that in one dream, a **BIG** tree was going to get chopped down.

With God's help, Daniel explained the king's dream. "This dream is about you," said Daniel. "Just like the tree, you're big and strong. But you're going to get cut down."

Daniel said that God was unhappy because King Nebbie tried to turn people away from God. So the dream meant the king wouldn't be king much longer. And sure enough—chop-chop—King Nebbie soon became plain old Nebbie.

Later on, Daniel worked for another king named Darius—a much shorter name. He was a nicer king, too. He liked Daniel. But others who worked for King Darius were jealous of Daniel, and they wanted to get him in trouble.

They made a plan. One worker said to the king, "You should make a law that for one month, no one can pray to anyone but you. You. You. You." That sounded like a good idea to Darius.

But all the workers knew that Daniel prayed to God three times a day. **One. Two. Three.**

And Daniel kept praying to God even after the new law passed. So the workers' mean trick worked: Daniel got in trouble with a capital *T*.

When he made his new law, King Darius didn't realize he would have to punish his good friend. *What was I thinking?* he asked himself. But the law couldn't be changed. Sadly, the king ordered his guards: "Throw Daniel into the *lions'* den."

Big, hungry lions were inside, waiting for their next meal.

"Daniel," said the king, "you broke a law when you prayed to God. I have to punish you. I'm sorry, and I hope your God saves you."

The king's guards threw Daniel into the lions' den. Then they pushed a huge rock in front of its opening to keep Daniel inside.

The lions **g-r-r-r-rowled** and looked at Daniel like he was lunchmeat. Daniel prayed, "God, help me. I'm scared. These lions are bigger than me."

King Darius couldn't sleep at all that night. But in the lions' den, an ANGEL had appeared. The angel held the big jaws of the lions closed—and kept them shut tight all night—so they couldn't hurt Daniel.

The next morning, the king rushed to the den.

"Move that stone!" he demanded.

The guards pushed the rock aside. The king yelled, "Daniel! Are you okay? Did your God save you from the lions?"

"Yes, I'm here!" Daniel answered.

Happy, the king demanded: "Get Daniel out of there right now!"

So, they freed Daniel. But things didn't work out too well for the workers who had tricked King Darius. He threw *them* into the lions' den. Now who felt like **lunchmeat?**

Did you know that God is always with you? Even when
you're scared, God is there. He is! God is bigger than any
grouchy king. He's bigger than mean, hungry lions.
He's **HUGE!**
   He can help when you get in trouble, just like He helped
Daniel. Just have faith in Him, and pray when you're scared.
God is stronger than the biggest rock. He'll take care of you.

Abraham & Isaac

6 NOW, THAT'S A LAUGH

❚ love this joke book. Hey! Listen to this one:

Q: What did the tall pyramid say to the flat pyramid?
A: You're missing the point!

Hee-hee! Proverbs 17:22 says, "A happy heart is like good medicine."

Laughing makes us feel good. Speaking of laughing, I've just remembered a happy story.

"Sarah!" Abraham called. "Why do shepherds sleep so well?"

"I don't know," answered Sarah. "Why?"

"Because they're always counting sheep!" Abraham threw his head back as he chuckled.

Then his eyes grew wide when he heard the Lord say, "I am God All-Powerful. You and Sarah are going to be parents!"

Abraham bowed before the Lord and smiled broadly as he said to himself, *This is the best* JOKE *of all. Me! A father! I'm nearly 100 years old—and Sarah's 90!*

Later the Lord visited Abraham again.

"In about a year, the son I promised you will be born," announced the Lord.

Sarah heard what God said, and she giggled.

"Why did Sarah laugh?" God asked.

Sarah gulped. "I-I didn't laugh."

"Yes you did!" the Lord said. "You think you're too old to have a son. But you'll see. And when he is born, name him Isaac" (which means 'he laughed').

Sure enough, a year later Sarah and Abraham held their newborn son. And they laughed with joy.

Abraham and Isaac spent a lot of time together. At night, the family sat around the campfire. And they ate sweet crackers dipped in chocolate and topped with gooey melted stuff.

"What are these things?" Isaac asked.

"I don't know, but they're good. Want **S'MORE?**" Abraham offered.

Some years later, the Lord told Abraham, "Take Isaac into the mountains and **sacrifice** him to Me."

Abraham placed his hands over his heart. "My own sweet son?" he whispered. "How can I do such a thing? But how can I not do what God has commanded? I will trust Him, and I will obey."

The next morning, Abraham packed the supplies he would need. He and Isaac took two servants and headed for the mountains.

"Hey, Dad!" Isaac said. "You said we're going into the mountains to offer a sacrifice to God, right?"

Abraham nodded his head.

"Well, then, didn't you forget something? Where's the lamb we're supposed to sacrifice?"

Abraham put his arm around Isaac's shoulder as they trudged up the mountain. "God Himself will supply the lamb. You'll see."

When they reached the place God had described, Abraham built an altar. Then he laid wood on top of it.

"Come here, Isaac," Abraham said. Isaac obeyed, and Abraham tied his son's hands and feet together.

"Am I the sacrifice God has provided?" Isaac asked.

"I am obeying God," Abraham answered. "I love God and trust Him. And I know He loves you, my son. We must **trust** Him together."

As Abraham prepared to sacrifice Isaac, the Lord spoke: "Abraham, stop! Don't kill your son or hurt him in any way. You have proved your trust in Me; you were willing to give Me your only son."

Happily, Abraham untied Isaac and helped him off the altar. "Look!" Abraham exclaimed. "A ram caught in the bushes!"

"God *did* supply the sacrifice," said Isaac.

Then the Lord said, "Because you trusted Me, your family will become as numerous as the STARS in the sky!"

Eventually, Isaac had his own children. Then Isaac's children had children, and *they* had even more children. Abraham's family is still growing!

God kept His PROMISE to Abraham because Abraham trusted Him. Proverbs 3:5 says to trust God with your whole heart! That's what Abraham did!

6

SOMETIMES LESS IS MORE

CRAAAASH!

Rats, I just broke my new pitcher. What a racket! I hope I didn't wake the neighbors. Looks like I'm going to have to find some glue.

You know, once in Bible times, the sound of **breaking** pitchers defeated an entire army.

"Ten thousand . . . twenty thousand . . . I love numbers," said Gideon. "Big **numbers** are my favorite, especially when I'm counting soldiers.

"Thirty-two thousand . . . But I bet we can find more. Those pesky Midianites won't stand a chance against this huge army."

"Gideon!" boomed a deep voice.

"God? Is that You?" Gideon replied.

"Your army is too big."

"But, Lord," Gideon said, "I was thinking of making it even bigger. Those Midianites take our barley bread, steal our toilet paper, and BLOW their noses on the *Israeli Times!*"

"Gideon!" God said. "Your army is too big. I don't want the Israelites to think *they* won the battle. I want them to know that *I* protected them."

Gideon gathered up his army. "Some of you have to go home. We've gotta trust God, and He wants a smaller army. So, whoever's wearing purple socks, go away."

Two men took off.

"If you like spinach, get lost."

Five more ran away.

"Okay! Who's **afraid** to fight in battle?"

Thousands of men scampered off—twenty-two thousand, to be exact.

"God," Gideon said, "we're down to ten thousand. Can we go to battle now?"

God said, "That's still too many."

"What?" cried Gideon. "The Midianites have lots of soldiers in their camp. Many, many, many soldiers."

"Trust Me, Gideon. You still need to make your army smaller. The next time your soldiers drink from the lake, watch. Some will kneel to drink; others will stand guard. Take those on the lookout into battle with you."

Gideon watched his soldiers by the water.

Do these guys think they're on vacation? he thought. *They're not looking at anything but the water! Anyone could sneak up on them!* Gideon marched over to those who failed the test.

"You, you, and you. Go home!" And on he went around the lake.

"God," called Gideon, "I'm down to three hundred."

"Perfect!" answered God. "Now go SPY on the Midianite camp. You'll see; I will take care of you."

Gideon crept up the hill. "Good gravy!" he whispered. "They must have a **bazillion** soldiers." Gideon heard two Midianites talking.

"What a nightmare!" said one soldier. "I dreamed that someone threw barley bread into our camp, and all our tents fell over. What could that mean?"

The other soldier replied, "It must mean that Gideon's army will defeat us!"

Gideon smiled and sneaked back to his troops.

"Quick! Everyone grab a trumpet, a pitcher, and a torch. Charge the enemy!" Gideon ordered.

When his soldiers reached the Midianite camp, they blew their trumpets and smashed their pitchers.

Gideon's soldiers made so much noise that they frightened away the Midianites. Some even yelled, "*Yikes!* Run! They've got pitchers! And trumpets! What if they throw barley bread?"

Gideon was wise to trust God. Sometimes, it seems like we don't have everything we need. Gideon THOUGHT he needed more soldiers to beat the Midianites. But he didn't.

So trust God. He'll always take care of you. In Psalms 28:7, the Bible says, "I trust Him, and He helps me."

BE MY BOYFRIEND, BOAZ

I know I hid some cheesy wheat crackers somewhere. I thought I left them in this closet, but all I can find in here are stinky sneakers. I'm so hungry I could eat a shoe—but not a stinky shoe.

Achoo! A stinky, wheaty shoe! Ew! Did my cheesy crackers turn back into wheat? Hay? Hey! This stuff reminds me of the story of Ruth.

Once, in Moab, there lived a friendly young widow named Ruth. One day, Ruth's mother-in-law, Naomi, came to her and said, "I'm leaving this place. May the Lord be kind to you since you've been so kind to me. **Adios, ciao, bye-bye.**"

"If you must go, fine," said Ruth. "But I'm coming with you. Where you go, I will go. Your friends will be my friends. And your God will be my God."

"If you insist," said Naomi. "Now let's blow this figsicle stand."

So Ruth and Naomi traveled to Bethlehem. When they arrived, people in the city called, "Naomi? Is that you? We haven't seen you in a camel's age!"

"I'm not Naomi anymore," said Naomi. "Naomi was happy. She had a husband and two sons. Now they've all passed away, and I'm **SAD.** Call me Mara now. It's a better name for a bitter woman."

Naomi looked up at the blue sky and asked, "God, did You forget to take care of me?"

When several days had passed, Ruth found a farm where she could gather wheat. It was owned by a man named Boaz, one of Naomi's relatives. All morning, Ruth worked behind his farmhands, gathering up the wheat they dropped. Boaz noticed Ruth and **STOPPeD** to watch her. "Who's she?" he asked.

A worker replied, "She's gathering food for that relative of yours."

"You mean Naomi," said Boaz. "The one who calls herself Mara."

Boaz waved at Ruth and went over to where she was working.
He cleared his throat. "I heard how nice you've been to my
relative Naomi. And I hope you'll come gather wheat anytime
you want."

"Thank you, **Brown Eyes.** Um, I mean Boaz." Ruth
replied. Her cheeks turned rosy red. She smiled and went back
to her work.

Boaz whispered to his workers, "Drop lots of wheat for Ruth.
Let her gather as much as she likes."

At home that evening, Naomi asked, "Ruth, where did you find all this wheat?"

"Oh, that," said Ruth. "From this totally sweet guy named Boaz. He was **SO♥O♥O** nice," Ruth beamed. "He had beautiful brown eyes!"

"Ruth!" cried Naomi. "Maybe you should marry him . . ."

"Me? Marry Boaz?" Ruth giggled. "What would I wear? What would I say? What would he say?"

"Don't worry," said Naomi. "I'll tell you what to do."

That night, after working in the wheat, Boaz snoozed in his field. Ruth tiptoed by his feet and crouched down. *Thump, thump, thump,* beat her heart.

"What's all that thumping?" Boaz mumbled as he stirred. "Oh Ruth! It's you!" cried Boaz. "You gave me a scare! I thought you were a tap-dancing goat at first. Why are you here so late?"

"Well," said Ruth. "I was wondering . . . would you take care of me? And my family?"

"You bet!" answered Boaz. And that's exactly what he did. Boaz and Ruth were married, and before long, God blessed them with a baby.

Naomi was so proud to be a nana. "Our little Obed's so perfect," she said as she HAPPILY bounced her grandbaby on her knee. "God *does* take care of us all."

Ruth gave them both a big hug.

Did you know that when little Obed grew up, he had a son named Jesse? And Jesse's son was David—who became King David, Israel's greatest king. How's that for planning ahead?

Ruth trusted God. He not only took care of her, but He also helped her take care of Naomi. And He **BLESSED** Boaz with a strong wife.

See? God's always thinking ahead—He always has a plan for us.

David & Goliath

6 LITTLE ROCKS, BIG BULLY

Hey, there! Don't let the armor fool you. It's me—Mr. Henry! And I'm prepared for battle. Well, almost prepared. I still need to find my sword—this armor just doesn't look right without it.

Aha! I bet I'll find swords in this trunk! Maybe even spears! It's sure to have arrows, shields, and . . . a slingshot?

What good is a slingshot? It's just a string of leather with a pouch in the middle. Well, as David discovered, it's a whole lot of good if you have to fight a giant. Let me tell you what happened.

Once there lived a boy named David. God loved him very much. God even blessed the boy with the courage of a soldier because He wanted to make David a king.

Young David worked in the fields, protecting his sheep. One night, a grizzly bear tried to ATTACK the sheep. But David jumped in the way. The bear growled at David. David growled right back at that bear.

"Put 'em up! Put 'em up!"

David fought with the bear and defeated it with his bare hands.

Much later, David went to work for King Saul, a ruler with a BAD attitude. The king did not realize God was preparing David to take over his kingdom. If he had, he would have booted David right out of his camp.

When King Saul was grouchy—which was all the time—David played music to cheer him up.

But one day, a loud and disturbing noise filled the countryside. It even drowned out David's music.

Boom. Boom. Boom. Boom!

A mean giant named Goliath stomped into view.

"You'll all be my slaves. You'll be cookin' my stew. You'll be lickin' my boots . . . unless you can find one person who will fight me."

"What are we going to do?" one soldier asked. "Who will fight Goliath? He's at least ten feet tall!"

When David heard the boastful giant, he asked, "Just who does Goliath think he is, threatening our buds?"

King Saul shook, afraid of the big creep. But David declared
he was ready to fight.

"Let me take him down!" said David.

The king agreed, but said, "First put on this suit of **ARMOR.**"
David scrambled into the metal clothes.

"I can't see," moaned David, staggering under the weight.

The king laughed. "Your helmet's too big!"

"Ooof. This weighs more than I do," David said, struggling
out of the armor. "I'll clobber that giant without it."

"Come out, come out, wherever you are, you rotten giant!" yelled David. "I'm not afraid of you."

BOOM. BOOM. BOOM. BOOM!

Goliath's feet shook the ground as he marched, madder than a mama bear, toward young David.

David had no sword or spear. Instead, he clutched his slingshot, a few rocks, and the courage God gave him.

From the crowd that had gathered, someone cried, "Is he nuts? He can't fight with just a slingshot! He needs an army."

The giant looked David over and smirked. "Hey, short-stuff!" The giant laughed. "You think you can fight me with a bunch of *Pebbles?*"

David declared, "I don't need a sword. My God will take care of me."

David loaded his slingshot. He spun the leather pouch over his head and let go of one string, flinging a rock at Goliath. That rock popped the giant right between the eyes!

Doink. And Goliath went out like a light.

"Whooa, hooo!" the army cheered. Freed from the giant, they picked up David and tossed him around in celebration.

"You should be our KING!" the crowd shouted.

And one day, David *would* be their king.

Isn't it awesome how God gave David the courage to fight the giant? David didn't need a suit of armor. He just needed his slingshot and God on his side.

I don't need this hunk of metal to be **brave,** either. My courage comes from God too. So if God wants me to fight a giant, I'll say, "Put 'em up! Put 'em up!"

SIMPLY SUPERB SUPERHERO

Most of the time I'm Mr. Henry. But today I'm—*ta da*—Super Henry! I'm brave! I'm strong! I'm not afraid to go to the dentist!

I found this superhero outfit in my costume box and thought it might give me courage. Then I realized how much courage it would take just to put on these tights! Now what should I do?

Maybe I should wear armor and ride a horse to the dentist. That's what a knight would do. What would a queen do? Oh, I know a queen who was really brave—Queen Esther. And look! Here's her CROWN!

When King Xerxes crowned Esther as his queen, he didn't know everything about her. Esther had a big secret. **SH-H-H!** She was Jewish!

Esther's Uncle Mordecai warned her not to tell anyone. "Our people have many enemies," he explained.

One of those enemies worked with the king. His name was Haman. (Like, "Hey, man! Get over here.")

"Hey-man" wanted people to worship him like a god.

"Everyone! Bow down to me," he commanded. "Bow
LOWER,
LOWER!
I can still see your eyebrows!"

But Esther's Uncle Mordecai refused. "I only worship the true
and living God," he said.

Haman's whole body shook with rage. "That Mordecai is a
Jew," he muttered. "I must find a way to get rid of him and *all*
of the Jews."

Haman got an idea. It involved telling the king a big **FIB.** "There are some people in your kingdom who don't obey your laws," Haman said. "I think you should make a law to destroy them!"

"Write the law and carry it out," the king declared.

So Haman wrote a new law. Because of it, all of the Jewish people would be destroyed on a certain day.

When Mordecai and the other Jews found out, they moaned like a bunch of skateboarders who crashed without kneepads.

Mordecai sobbed loudly outside the palace. When Queen Esther heard him, she asked, "What's wrong?"

"You must talk to the king!" he pleaded. "Or we will all die!"

"I can't!" Esther replied in fear. "It's against the law to go to the king unless he has sent for you. He could have me killed!"

"Perhaps you were chosen to be queen for this reason," said Mordecai. "You must use your position to save your people."

"I'll need God's strength," she said. "Ask everyone to **FAST** and pray. Then I will go to the king, even though I may die."

After Esther and the people prayed, she put on her best dress. *I hope the king's in a good mood today,* she thought.

She walked toward the throne room and took a deep breath.

"You can't go in there," a guard bellowed. "The king hasn't called for you!"

Just then, the king saw Esther in the doorway. He smiled and said, "Esther, my queen! What do you need?"

Esther smiled too, and sighed with relief. *Whew!*

She said, "I have planned a yummy dinner party. Would you and Haman please come?"

Haman overheard the queen's invitation and nearly jumped up and down. He ran home to his wife and boasted, "Guess who's invited to Queen Esther's party? Me! No one else but me—and the king, of course!"

At the party, King Xerxes and Haman enjoyed their Babaloney sandwiches. Then the king said, "Okay, Esther, tell me the **REAL** reason you invited us here tonight."

Queen Esther pleaded, "If I please you, O King, let me live. And let my people live, too." The king grabbed Esther's hands.

"What are you saying?" he asked. "Who would dare harm you?"

"The man who wrote a new law that will kill all Jews!" Esther told him. "Your wicked servant Haman!"

"Guards!" the king roared. "Seize this man! We will deal with him like we do with all **TRAITORS!**"

"Let us write a new law to protect the Jews!" the king said to his queen.

God gave Esther the courage and strength to speak up and save her people. And when *we* need courage, all we have to do is ask God to help us. The Bible promises that we can do all things through Christ who gives us strength. I'm just glad we don't have to wear superhero outfits to make us brave!

6 TAKE THE HEAT

Twang. Twang. Twang.

Yuck. This banjo sounds like a broken doorbell. It's out of tune, and it must be a bazillion years old. And I have a recital tonight! I'll have to stand up and play in front of loads of people. How scary!

This reminds me of a story about three young men who courageously stood up for God when they heard another musical instrument play . . .

King Nebuchadnezzar (you remember King Nebbie, don't you?) searched all over for perfect workers. He wanted dudes with good looks, strength, and brains.

He soon found Shadrach, Meshach, and Abednego. Shadrach had great hair and perfect teeth. Meshach could bench-press four hundred pounds. And Abednego could recite the entire dictionary, from *aardvark* to *zucchini*. Together they formed the perfect TEAM.

So King Nebbie said, "Dudes, you're hired."

One day, King Nebbie bossed around some of his workers.

"My new STATUE isn't big enough," the king grumbled. "Make Goldie huge. Gigantic. With a big, honkin' head."

King Nebbie planned to make everyone bow down and worship this statue.

I know! the king thought. *I'll make my workers play a game of Nebbie Says. Because what Nebbie says goes—if I do say so myself.*

Before long, King Nebbie called everyone to the river, including Shadrach, Meshach, and Abednego.

The king yelled out the rules: "It's time to play Nebbie Says. I'm Nebbie. So do what I say. When you hear the zithers, trumpets, flutes, and kazoos, fall down and worship Goldie. If anyone refuses, I will throw him into the blazing furnace. And it's hot, hot, hot!"

The crowd trembled.

"Did he say 'blazing furnace'?"

"Who is this Goldie?" Shadrach asked his friends. "You know we can't bow to a statue."

"For real," Meshach echoed. "We only **BOW** down to God. Goldie isn't God. I could fling that metal-head across the river!"

"Meshach, he's nine feet wide," said Shadrach.

Abednego chimed in, "And almost a hundred feet tall. Hey, according to my dictionary, *furnace* means 'an extremely hot place.' Will they really throw us inside if we don't bow down?"

Just then, the music began to play. *Twang. Twang. Twang.*

"Nebbie says: Bow down now, town!" shouted the king.

Immediately, all the people plopped to their knees and bowed to Goldie.

That is, all the people but Shadrach, Meshach, and Abednego. They stood courageously. They didn't even slouch.

King Nebbie blew his top. His crown flew right off his head.

"Just who do you think you are, disobeying my command?!" he demanded. "Bow now, or I'll throw you into the furnace. No god can save you from *my* power!"

They could see that the furnace burned hotter than a solar flare. Still, Shadrach declared, "We will not bow to your **fake** god. He *is* fake, by the way. We worship the *real* God. Between God and Goldie, there's no contest. God wins."

"Soldiers!" the king howled. "Tie these disobedient dudes up, and throw them into the furnace!"

The crowd watched anxiously. Then they watched in amazement. They could see the three men just walking around in that hot furnace. Or did they see four men? Hmmm.

The king leaped toward the furnace.

God had sent an ANGEL to rescue His three faithful men. They marched right out of the fire, unharmed. Not roasted like marshmallows. Not even burnt like toast.

Impressed, the king said, "These guys didn't follow the rules of Nebbie Says. And their God saved them. So, here's a new rule. Nobody—and I mean nobody—can say anything bad about their God. Or I'll huff, and I'll puff, and I'll blow your house down."

Wow! What brave young men! Shadrach, Meshach, and Abednego were also smart. They knew God would take care of them, so they weren't afraid to do what was right. They stood **STRONG** for God.

I'm going to pray that God gives me just a little of this kind of courage when I play at my recital tonight.

Twang. Twang. Twang.

I think I sound better already!

6 MOM KNOWS BEST

Dear Lord, I love to pray to You. Please help me tell others about You. I want to help them understand how wonderful You are. Show me the best way to do this. Thank You. Amen.

Well, hi there! See this **COAT?** It belonged to the great prophet Samuel. His mom, Hannah, made it for him. Of course, he was a kid at the time. Talk about an answer to prayer! God answered Hannah's prayer by giving her Samuel.

Elkanah and his wife, Hannah, lived back in Bible times. People often said, "They're such a cute couple. Too bad they don't have any children."

But these words made Hannah sad. One day, Elkanah came home from work early and found Hannah crying.

"What is it, my little sweetie pie?" he asked.

"I want a baby of my own," Hannah sobbed. "I want to kiss his little toes and rock him to sleep at night."

Elkanah hugged Hannah. "But **sugarplum,** you have me! What more could you want?"

He plopped down next to her and yanked off his sandals. "Here," he said, "you can kiss *my* toes!"

Hannah chuckled and held her nose. "I do love you, but please put your sandals back on. I think I'd rather pack for our trip than kiss your toes."

Every year Elkanah and Hannah traveled to the temple in Shiloh. They worshiped God there. Hannah usually looked forward to their trips. But this year she had a lot on her mind.

"I can't stop thinking about having a baby," she said to herself.

When they reached Shiloh, they entered the **banquet** hall. Elkanah's eyes grew big. "Hannah, my little cupcake, look at all this food!"

But Hannah still felt sad. She didn't eat a bite all night long.

Later that evening, Hannah went for a walk. As she walked, she prayed softly: "God, if You will give me a child, I promise to give him back to You. He will serve You all his life."

Eli, the priest, watched her. He saw her lips moving, but he couldn't hear any words. "OY VEY!" Eli groaned. "That woman is acting quite strange."

He approached Hannah and cleared his throat. "What are you doing out here all alone—talking to yourself?"

Hannah looked up, startled by the priest's question.

"I'm not talking to myself, sir," she said.

"Well, what's wrong with you?" asked Eli.

"I am a troubled woman," answered Hannah. "I'm telling the Lord all my problems. I've been so very sad that all I can do is pray."

Eli smiled. "Forgive me, dear woman. Go in *peace,* and may God answer your prayer."

Hannah skipped back to the banquet hall, singing a song of praise. Elkanah watched as she danced through the doorway.

"There you are, my little biscuit!" he said. "And you're smiling!" he added happily.

She wiggled in beside him. "I am so hungry, I could eat a camel."

"Camel? I'm sorry—no camel on the menu tonight! How about ice cream with some **grapes** and **pickles?** Slow down, my little peach cake! I've never seen you eat like this. That must have been some walk!"

Hannah told Elkanah about her prayer. "I believe God will answer my prayer and give us a son," she said.

Many months later, Samuel was born. What joy! When Samuel was old enough, his parents took him to Shiloh.

"This is our son, Samuel," Hannah said to Eli. "To honor the PROMiSE I made to God, we have brought him to live with you in the temple."

Then she turned to Samuel and said, "We love you. We'll visit you often, and I'll make you a new coat every year."

Samuel had a happy life in the temple. He grew, and he learned. Eventually he became one of God's prophets. And God blessed Hannah and Elkanah with more children.

You know, I just realized that God has answered my prayer, too. God made me a storyteller, and that's one way I can tell people about Him. I just *love* telling stories. Can you tell?

Elisha & the Boy
POWER OF PRAYER

Yikes! My power went out. And I was right in the middle of writing a story. Hope I can remember it later!

I always keep my oil lamp filled, just for emergencies like this one. Too bad my computer doesn't run on oil . . .

I know, I'll pray to God for help in remembering my story ideas. I'm sure He'll help. Maybe He'll even help me think of better ones.

Prayer really **WORKS**—as Elisha, one of God's prophets, knew well.

One day, Elisha traveled to a city called Shunem. There, he met an important woman.

"Elisha! I've heard that you're a prophet," she said. "You simply *must* come to dinner tonight and meet my husband."

Elisha agreed to come.

"YUMMERS!" he said as he licked his fingers after dinner.

Elisha soon became a regular for their Friday all-you-can-eat fish fry!

"Darling," the woman said to her husband one afternoon. "I think it's positively wonderful that a **prophet** dines with us every week. Wouldn't it be even more exciting if he stayed with us when he's in town? Maybe we should make a room for him on the roof."

Her husband peered at her over his scroll. "Whatever you want, sweet'ums."

The next week, the woman showed Elisha the new room.

"Wow!" Elisha exclaimed. "What a generous gift! Thank you!"

Later, Elisha said to his servant, Gehazi, "I must find a way to properly **THaNK** this woman for her kindness. What should I give her?"

"Hmm," Gehazi said. "She already has a toaster, fancy dishes, and—you won't believe it—*two* camel-drawn carriages."

"Is there anything she *doesn't* have?" Elisha asked.

"Well, she doesn't have a son," Gehazi answered.

Elisha sent for the woman. "Have I got a 𝒮𝒰ℛ𝒫ℛℐ𝒮ℰ for you! By this time next year, you'll be holding a bouncing baby boy."

The woman's mouth dropped open. "No way!" she said. "Are you serious?"

Sure enough, the woman gave birth to a son.

"Look, darling," the woman said to her husband. "He's got your double chin!"

Their baby grew into a happy little boy.

But a few years later, the boy got sick and died. His mother carried him upstairs and laid him on Elisha's bed.

When she came back downstairs, she said to her husband, "Send a servant to me with a donkey. I'm going to Mount Carmel to find Elisha."

So the woman and the servant *raced* off.

As they approached Mount Carmel, Elisha spotted them in the distance. He said to Gehazi, "Quick! Go meet the woman and find out what's wrong!"

After the woman told Elisha about her son, Elisha said to Gehazi, "Run to the boy and take my **walking stick.** Don't talk to anyone on the way. Lay the stick across the boy's face."

But the woman wouldn't go home unless Elisha went with her. When they arrived, they found the boy was still dead, even though Gehazi had followed Elisha's instructions.

Elisha went into the room and shut the door. He prayed for God's help. Then he **stretched** out over the boy— eyeball-to-eyeball, nose-to-nose, hand-to-hand. The child's skin became warm. Then he sneezed seven times! Elisha got up and smiled.

When the boy's mother rushed into the room, she bowed at Elisha's feet. Then she picked up her son and gave him a big hug.

Hey, the power came back on! It's so much easier to write my stories with electricity. Thank You, Lord.

You know, God always hears our prayers. And He always answers our prayers too (though sometimes His answer is no).

When the Lord answered Elisha's prayer, He helped Elisha bring a boy back to life. Now that's DiVINE power!

Cain & Abel

BAD BOY, BAD BOY

Aunt Thelma's birthday is tomorrow. What should I give her? She loves slippers, but this Game Blaster 5000 is soooo COOL! It's got 3-D graphics and virtual surround sound. And it's nuclear powered so I—er—she can play practically forever.

   I can't decide which gift to give her. Hmmm. I wonder how Cain and Abel decided what gifts to give God?

Cain and Abel were Adam and Eve's very first children. They did everything together—home school, chores, and one-on-one basketball. They even played tag.

"You're *it!*" Cain yelled as he took off running.

When Abel caught up with him, he said, "You know what, Cain? You're my favorite brother!"

Cain rolled his eyes. "I'm your *only* brother, Abel!"

One night, Adam listened as the boys said their prayers. "Dear God," said Abel, "thank You for giving me such a cool brother."

"Yeah!" said Cain. "And thank You for giving *me* such a cool brother. Please help me to be better than him—um, I mean, please help me to be a better person *like* him."

"It's good to thank God," Adam explained. "It's also good to give Him **GiFTS** to show Him our love and thanks."

Cain and Abel thought about their father's words as they drifted off to sleep.

When the boys grew older, Abel became a shepherd, and Cain took up farming. One day, Abel took his sheep to the pasture. He spotted his **favorite** little lamb. After watching it for a long time, he smiled and said, "I want to give this lamb to God so He will know how much I love Him."

So Abel brought the little lamb to God's altar. God said, "I accept this loving gift, Abel. But most of all, I appreciate your loving heart."

Abel beamed with happiness.

"Too bad. This lettuce looks wilted," Cain thought. "Hey! I know! I'll sacrifice this lettuce and some other vegetables to God."

When Cain brought his less-than-perfect produce to God's altar, God sighed. "Cain, you shouldn't have."

"Aw," Cain replied, "it was nothing—really!"

"I know," answered God. "That's the problem. A gift given without love is empty—*worthless*."

Embarrassed by the truth, Cain jumped up and down on his basket, yelling, "I always knew you liked Abel better than me!"

God answered, "If you truly loved Me, you would have chosen a gift you knew I would like. Then I would have accepted your **OFFERiNG**."

Cain kicked his basket as far as he could.

"Your jealousy will get you into trouble someday," God warned. "Do not let sin control you."

Cain turned away from God and stormed home. He saw Abel in the yard. "Hey, Abel!" he **snarled.** "I wanna talk to you!"

Cain charged down the path, and Abel followed. "What's wrong, Cain?" Abel called out. "Did I do something?"

Suddenly Cain turned and grabbed Abel. "Yes!" he bellowed. "*You* are the reason God turned away from me!"

"But Cain . . ." Abel began.

Without another word, Cain clobbered his brother. And Abel fell lifeless to the ground. Cain walked off without looking back.

A while later, God asked him, "Where is your brother, Abel?" Cain answered, "How should I know? I'm not his baby-sitter." "Oh, Cain," God said. "Look what you've done. You've **killed** your brother with your own hands. Because of this, you will work the ground, but no crops will grow. Worse than that, you will be separated from Me because of your sin."

If Cain had truly loved God, he would have also loved his brother. But jealousy, not love, filled Cain's heart.

Do you ever feel jealous of someone? If so, try praying. The Bible says to "have true love for your brothers. So love each other deeply with all your heart" (1 Peter 1:22).

I love my Aunt Thelma. And now that I think about it, I've known all along what to give her for her birthday— cozy SLIPPERS. I know they'll make her happy.

Jacob & Esau

A BOWL OF BIRTHRIGHT STEW

I just got a letter from Professor Henry, my brilliant brother. He's a famous archaeologist. I wish he could be here to share this pot of veggie soup with me today.

My brother and I are best friends. Sometimes we play JOKES on each other. Like one time, I hid his new shovel on the roof. And another time, he glued a big, red mustache on Bubbles's fishbowl.

But I remember a pair of brothers in the Bible whose behavior wasn't so brotherly . . .

Rebekah and Isaac wanted a family. One day Rebekah announced, "We're having twins! And God told me that the second born would rule over the first!"

"That's odd," said Isaac. "You know the birthright and blessing belong to the firstborn."

Usually, the first son receives a double portion of his father's money—his **"birthright"**—and a special blessing. The first son also grows up to become the family's spiritual leader.

A few months later, Rebekah gave birth to **twins.** The first boy, Esau, had lots and lots of hair. His brother, Jacob, did not.

Esau grew up and became a hunter and so won his father's heart. He also got much hairier. Jacob, his mother's favorite, became a cook. He never grew much hair.

Despite his mother's love, Jacob felt jealous of Esau. "I deserve the birthright," Jacob said to himself.

One day Esau marched off singing, "A-hunting I will go.
A-hunting I will go . . ."

But a few days later, he came home empty-handed and
hungry. "Oooh, yummy. What's that smell?" he asked.

"I call it 'CATcH SOUP,'" Jacob answered.

"What's the 'catch'?" asked Esau.

"You can have a bowl of soup, if you give me your birthright."

Esau thought for a second. Then his belly grumbled—loudly!
"Okay, it's a deal—my birthright for your soup."

Years later, Isaac had grown old and become nearly blind. He called for Esau. "It's time for you to receive your blessing," he said. "But first, I'd like you to go hunting. I want something tasty to eat."

"Yes sir!" shouted Esau. He ran off singing, "A-hunting I will go. A-hunting I will go. I'll get my dad some tasty meat; a BLESSING he'll bestow!"

Rebekah overheard them and grabbed Jacob. "Your father plans to give Esau *your* blessing—today! We have to act fast.

"Go and fetch a couple of goats," Rebekah continued. "I'll stoke up the fire and make some barbecue sauce. When you serve the meat to your father, he'll give *you* the blessing."

"Clever plan—except for one thing," said Jacob. "My arms are as smooth as silk. Dad will know it's me, and I'll get in trouble."

Rebekah smiled. "Don't worry. I have an idea. If you get caught, I'll take the **blame.** Now hurry!"

Rebekah covered Jacob with goatskins and gave him Esau's clothes, and Jacob took the meal to his father.

Isaac said, "Come closer so I can touch you." He reached out and felt the hair on Jacob's arms. He sniffed his clothes.

"You feel like Esau. And you sure smell like him. But you SOUND like Jacob," Isaac said doubtfully.

After his meal, Isaac blessed Jacob. "May God give you lots of good things. And may you rule wisely over the family."

Later, Esau burst in with a tray. "Dinner's ready, Dad," he said.
"What do you mean?" said Isaac. "I just finished eating. And, I already gave you my blessing."

"Oh no!" cried Esau. "That wasn't me. It was Jacob! He tricked me out of my birthright, and now he's stolen my blessing!"

When Rebekah saw how angry Esau was, she ran and found Jacob. "Get out of town!" she cried. "Find our relatives and stay with them for your own safety." And that's exactly what he did.

Out of jealousy, Jacob tricked his brother and his dad. And that jealousy cost his family something special—the chance to be **together.**

It's great being best friends with my brother. We love each other whether we're together or far apart.

And that package of dirt I mailed him yesterday, well, that was all in fun.

Prodigal Son
COME HOME, LITTLE PIGGY

Piggy, where art thou? Wherefore art thou, Piggy? Now, I mean it! Come on home, little Piggy! Wee, wee, wee, wee! All the way home!

I sure hope he hasn't **run away.** Maybe he went to market for roast beef. That's his favorite, you know. I'll just put some in his piggy dish. He can probably smell it clear across town with his big, honkin' nostrils. That should bring him home.

Say, this reminds me of someone else who ran away . . .

There once lived a man who had two sons. His boys were as different as night and day. One son said, "tah-*may*-toe"; the other one said, "tah-*mah*-toe."

One son said, "I love working on our ranch." But the other one said, "Working the farm is soooo boring. I'm outta here!"

So the Prodigal Son went to his dad. "Hey, Dad!" he said. "Can I have my **inheritance** now? I want to go hang at the beach."

This hurt the father very much. But he honored his son's wishes and gave him some money.

The Prodigal Son partied hearty. "I'm so cool, I gotta wear shades." And he bought new shades. Five pairs.

Surfer dudes crawled out of the sand to be his friends.

"You're so radical, dude!" said one surfer. "I'm craving an orange Slurpee. Spare me some coinage?"

"Sure, dude!" said the Prodigal Son. "Slurpees for everyone! Who wants a souvenir cup?"

Before long, the Prodigal Son realized he'd spent all his money.

"Whoa, baby!" he said. "I'm flat broke!"

"As in *busted*?" cried a surfer. "Bankrupt, like every other surfer on the beach? Later!"

The Prodigal Son's so-called friends disappeared faster than his money had.

A famine spread through the land, so finding macaroni got rough-a-roni. The Prodigal Son looked for a job. Only one place needed help: a pig farm. So he worked all day in the mud with oinkers, feeding them slop. Meals didn't come with his new job. Before long, even the pig slop started to look good to the Prodigal Son.

Am I out of my surfer-dude mind? he wondered. *My father's servants eat roast beef and ice cream. I should ask my father to hire me! But what if he won't forgive me?*

Back at home, the father prayed for his wandering son.

"He's not coming back, Dad!" the obedient son said.

"Son, I must pray for your brother," Dad explained. "There's a **famine** out there, and there's no work in the fields."

"Well, he sure didn't want to work here," his son pointed out. "But I stayed—I'm on the ball. And did I mention that I'm charming?"

"You're not very charming right now," the father said. Suddenly, he spotted his Prodigal Son trudging up the road.

"You're home!" yelled Dad as he ran to his son. The not-so-charming son muttered, "I'll bet he's just here to refill his wallet."

The father cried as he gave his smelly boy a hug. "My son! You've come home."

The Prodigal Son hung his head. "I'm too crummy to be called your son. I ran away to have FUN. But the fun ran away with my money. I'm so sorry, Dad. I didn't mean to hurt you."

"All is forgiven," said Dad. "I'm glad you came home."

The father threw a whopping party, complete with roast beef and ice cream. No pig slop. Meanwhile, his other son moped.

"Son, why are you **POUTiNG?**" asked the father. "Your brother has returned safely."

"He ran off, blew all that money, and *he* gets a party! Is that what *I* have to do to get attention around here?"

"Son," the father said gently, "everything I have is yours. I felt like your brother was dead. Gone forever. Now I'm rejoicing because he's come back to us!"

Isn't it awesome how the Prodigal Son's father forgave him? Even after the boy hurt his father's feelings, his dad still loved him.

When we mess up, God forgives us too. All we have to do is show we're sorry. He loves us and forgives us. He's always ready to listen. And He wants us to forgive others.

Now, if only Piggy would come home . . . Wait! Did you hear an *oink?*

I CAN SEE CLEARLY NOW

I know I put a Damascus road map in here somewhere. It's ancient, so I should have filed it under "DO NOT LOSE." Now I can't find it.

I'll never forgive myself if I've lost it.

Wait a minute . . . God wants us to forgive *everybody*—including ourselves—no matter what. Even if we're grumpy, forgetful, or mean.

Let me tell you a story about a meanie who *really* needed God's forgiveness.

When Saul stormed around and made demands, people did what he wanted. Then they got out of his way.

"Watch out!" a man said to his friend. "Saul's cranky again. I think his belt is too tight!"

She muttered back, "Maybe his sandals are too small, and his feet hurt."

The truth was, Saul **hated** Christians. He even had his own army of Christian haters.

Once Saul's army tromped toward Damascus, looking for Christians. Saul wanted to throw them in jail.

His soldiers grinned. "What a beautiful day to bully Christians!"

Suddenly, a BRIGHT light blinded Saul. He heard a voice say, "Saul, Saul! Why are you doing things against Me?"

"Wh-who are you?" Saul asked.

"I am Jesus. I am the One you are trying to hurt."

"Who said that?" his soldiers whispered. "I don't see anyone!" Frightened, they grabbed Saul and ran to Damascus.

In Damascus, a man named Ananias sat eating his lunch. As he chowed down on his lentil soup, the Lord said to him: "Go to Saul. He's seen a vision in which you heal his blindness."

"What?" Ananias cried, spraying his soup. "Lord, are You talking about *the* Saul? The one who hates Christians? You want me to go to *him*?"

"That's the one," said the Lord. "I've got a special plan for him."

"Relax," Ananias told himself as he mopped his mess up. "Trust the Lord."

Though he was frightened, Ananias went looking for Saul.

"I'll believe it when I see it," Ananias muttered to himself. "Imagine! Saul, not hating Christians!"

Ananias found the right house and saw Saul slumped in a chair. Taking a deep breath, Ananias reached out and put his hands on Saul. He said, "Saul, God sent me. He is the One you saw on the road. He sent me to pray for you. The Lord will restore your SIGHT."

Immediately Saul could see again.

Saul stayed with Jesus' followers in Damascus for a while. When other Christians first spotted Saul, they cried, "Oh no! Here comes that creep Saul. Run for your lives!"

But Saul went into a synagogue and stood in the center. There he proclaimed, "Jesus *is* the Son of God!"

"Whoa!" gasped a Christian. "Did I just hear what I thought I heard? Didn't this guy used to hate us?"

Saul continued to talk about Jesus. Everyone listened—amazed by the change in him.

Next, Saul traveled to Jerusalem to visit more believers. But when they saw him, they ran.

"There's Saul, the 'mean machine,'" one man warned. "Stay away from him. He's **Trouble** with a capital *T*."

But Barnabas heard Saul's words.

"Wait a minute," Barnabas said. "I believe Saul has changed!"

He walked over to Saul with a smile. "Greetings, my friend. Let me introduce you to Jesus' disciples. They'll want to hear your story."

The disciples and other believers forgave Saul for being a meanie. "Go for it!" they cheered. "Tell your story!"

And Saul did!

Then one day the Holy Spirit told some of Jesus' disciples, "Send Saul and Barnabas as my **missionaries.** They can preach to people who haven't heard about me!"

Soon after, God changed Saul's name to Paul. No longer did people call him "Saul, the mean machine." Instead, he became known as "Paul, the preaching machine!"

You see, with God's help even **meanies** can change! If Ananias and the other believers can forgive mean people, so can we.

God's Word says, "Be kind and loving to each other. Forgive each other just as God forgave you in Christ" (Ephesians 4:32).

And even if I *never* find that map, I can forgive myself too.

6 A MATCH MADE IN HEAVEN

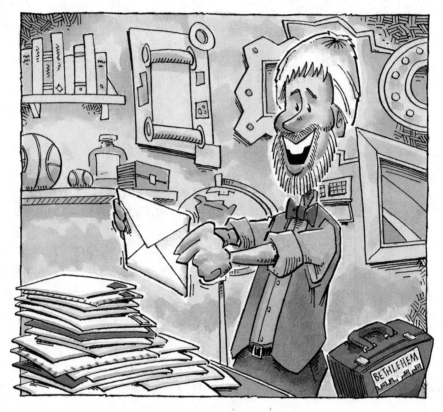

Look at all this junk mail! Coupons for "Meatless Swedish Meatballs" and a "Vacation for Two in Hullabaloo"! Good grief!

Wait a minute. Check this out! It's a birth announcement. My niece and her husband had a baby girl. And they named her Henrietta—after me!

This note says they want me to come visit. I guess I'd better hurry and buy my plane tickets. Driving takes too long.

Speaking of taking too long, I know a story about a young couple who walked a *looooonnnnngggg* way to a hillside city.

Mary and Joseph had begun to plan their **WEDDING.** They had plenty of time. It was still a year away.

"I definitely want lilies," Mary said. "And lots of roses."

Joseph closed his eyes and rubbed his belly. "Make sure there's lots of good stuff to eat—a big banquet—the works!"

"Oh! And cake," Mary added.

"Yeah, and cookies and ice cream and . . ."

Mary raised an eyebrow, and Joseph shrugged. "Well, I'm hungry!"

One day, the angel Gabriel appeared to Mary.

She barely glanced at him. "Oh good, you're here!" she said. "We love the olive and pimento dip idea. But we're not too keen on the grapes stuffed with pomegranate seeds."

"Hello?" Gabriel said.

Mary looked up. "You're not the caterer! Y-you're an angel!"

"Don't be afraid, Mary. I have a message from God. Although you're a **VIRGIN,** you will soon have a baby boy. God will be His Father. Name Him Jesus; many will call Him the Son of God."

Mary quickly told Joseph the news. But when she left, he GASPED, "Mary's going to have a baby?"

Upset, he fell onto his bed and buried his head in the pillow. "She can't have a baby! We're not married yet. Maybe I should just break up with her."

He drifted off to troubled sleep. In his dream, he saw an angel of the Lord.

"Hey, Joseph!" said the angel. "Don't break up with Mary. Everything she told you is true. The baby is from God."

When Joseph woke up, he ran to Mary's house.

"Mary!" he yelled. "I don't have to break up with you!"

"You were going to break up with me?"

"Well, yeah," Joseph confessed. "But then an angel told me that everything you said was true!"

"You didn't believe me?" Mary's face reddened.

"Well, it did sound a little strange. But I believe you now. Honest!"

"Okay," she said. Mary smiled. "Time for a big bear hug."

Months later, Joseph ran to Mary's garden. "I just heard," he said, panting, "that Caesar Augustus wants us all to go back to the city of our ancestors so he can do a head count!"

"Oh no! You mean we have to go to **Bethlehem?**" asked Mary. She rubbed her growing belly. "Let's see . . . Bethlehem is eighty miles away. If we walk one and a half miles an hour for six hours—with plenty of rest stops—that's nine miles a day. Divide that into—"

"It'll take us nine or ten days," Joseph interrupted.

"Honey, did you forget that I'm having a baby?" Mary asked.

"We'll be okay," Joseph assured her. "God will take care of us."

So Mary, Joseph, and their donkey packed their things. They knew the roads to Bethlehem would be crowded, so they packed carefully. Water, hay, and chicken salad on pita bread. Then they headed up the busy road.

Good-bye for now, Galilee!

When Mary and Joseph arrived in Bethlehem, Mary looked around. "Wow. This town is smaller than I thought it would be."

"I can't believe this is where King David was born," said Joseph.

Mary sighed. "And this is where God's Son will be born."

Joseph held Mary's hand and repeated the Scriptures he had learned as a child. "The prophet Micah said, 'But you, Bethlehem . . . are one of the SMALLEST towns in Judah.'"

"'But *from* you,'" continued Mary, "'will come One who will rule Israel for Me.'" (Micah 5:2)

Wow! Imagine that! Long before Mary and Joseph were born, God had already chosen the exact time and place for His Son to come to earth. God knows exactly when and where everyone will be born—including my new niece, Henrietta, and you and *your* children!

It's good to know nothing surprises God. *Everything* happens according to His **PLAN.**

Speaking of plans, I'd better start packing for my trip!

6 GOOD NEWS FOR ALL

I can't wait to see my niece's baby girl, my precious little Henrietta! You know, her parents couldn't have chosen a better name.

My niece and her husband sent out cards to tell people about their new baby. The cards give her name, her birth date, and how much she weighed. Her parents also sent a picture. Isn't she *lovely*?

When Jesus was born, God didn't send cards or pictures. He told the world in an even better way!

When Mary and Joseph got to Bethlehem, they headed straight for the inn. But it was jam-packed! Joseph finally elbowed his way to the innkeeper.

"We need a room!" he yelled above the noise.

"**NO ROOM!**" the innkeeper yelled back.

"My wife's going to have a baby!" pleaded Joseph.

"You should've called ahead," said the innkeeper.

But the innkeeper's wife said, "Oh! You poor things. We have some room in the stable. You can sleep there tonight."

Mary and Joseph led their donkey to the **stable**—a dark cave carved into the hillside.

"It's gloomy in here," said Mary. She shivered.

"Don't worry, dumpling," said Joseph. "At least we have shelter from rain or sleet or hail."

"Or lions or tigers or bears?" asked Mary.

"Yes. I think so," said Joseph. "Well, bears at least. They generally prefer berries or honey or fish—"

"Oh my," said Mary.

"The stable will give us some privacy," said Joseph. "If you can call sharing a room with animals 'private'!"

"Oh, the sheep aren't so baa-a-a-d," Mary joked.

"And we can make a bed out of straw," Joseph suggested.

"Good idea!" Mary looked around. "That manger will make a perfect crib."

"Crib!" Joseph said in alarm. "Do you think we'll need a crib tonight?"

"Yes," groaned Mary.

A loud cry startled the animals awake. Baby Jesus had arrived!

"He's beautiful," said Mary.

"His lungs work. That's for sure," said Joseph.

The innkeeper's wife heard baby Jesus' cries. She came into the stable carrying some clean cloths. "Let's get Him cleaned up," she offered. Then she gently took Him from Mary.

"Why! He's PERFECT!" she said. "Simply perfect."

Joseph looked at Mary. "She has *no* idea!" he whispered with a knowing smile.

Outside, the sky lit up. Shepherds jumped to their feet.
"Who turned on the sun?" yelled one shepherd in confusion.
"Look! ANGELS!" cried another. "Everywhere!"
"Don't be afraid!" An angel's voice boomed. "I bring good news—joyful news for all people."
The shepherds listened, amazed.
"Today," said the angel, "your Savior was born. He is Christ, the Lord. Born in David's town, you will find a baby wrapped in swaddling cloths. He's lying in a manger."

The angels praised God: "Let there be peace and goodwill for everyone! Glory to God in heaven!"

The shepherds laughed and cried and hugged each other. "Let's go to Bethlehem and find our Savior!" they said.

"What *is* a **Savior?**" asked the youngest shepherd.

His brother explained, "A Savior saves you. He's our new King!"

"Can shepherds visit a King?" asked the young shepherd.

"Of course!" said his brother. "The angels told us where to find Him. They *want* us to visit Him."

So the **SHEPHERDS** went to Bethlehem. "If I were a manger, where would I be?" wondered the youngest shepherd.

"In a stable like that one," said his brother. He pointed straight ahead.

Joseph watched the shepherds enter the stable. "Why did you come from the hills at night, leaving all your sheep?" he asked.

"To see our Savior," answered the shepherds. "The angels told us to come." And the shepherds told everyone how the angels had filled the sky.

God sent angels to tell the world about His Son's birth. His
message brought joy to the shepherds and to Mary and
Joseph. They knew Jesus would give **HOPE** to everyone . . .
for all time.

Isn't that a special gift?

God gave us another special gift, the Bible—God's Word.
It contains all of His stories . . . stories about His children, for
His children. Aren't you glad you're God's child?

THREE WISE MEN & A BABY

I'm ready to visit my brand-new niece, Henrietta. I even have a gift for her—a brand-new Bible. Oh, I know she can't read yet. But when Henrietta's older, she'll know the value of this gift.

People gave baby Jesus wonderful gifts too. In fact, there's a Bible story about three special gifts that Jesus received.

Three wise men followed a 𝒮𝒯𝒜ℛ to Jerusalem.

"Where's the new King?" they asked.

"Slippers fit for a king!" cried a woman. "I've got all sizes."

"Kingfish! Get your kingfish here!" called a boy. "Freshly caught!"

"No kingfish! No kingly shoes!" said a wise man. "We're looking for the King of the Jews."

"Uh-oh," whispered a castle spy, hiding nearby. "King Herod's not going to like this!"

"Y-your h-highness," began the spy. "**Strangers** in town claim a new King has been born."

"What?" Herod bellowed. "I'm the only king. Can there be two of me? I don't see two of me. I'm the only me. I'm the only king!"

"Oh, without a doubt, your majesty," said the spy.

"I bet this new 'king' wants to be me! He'll try to steal my throne," said Herod. "I'd better not take any chances. Find me this other 'king.'"

"King Herod called a meeting," said a man from Jerusalem. "No one knows who the new King is."

"There is no new king!" declared Herod. He gathered his priests and teachers. "Just find that bothersome baby. Where was He born?"

A priest answered, "The Scriptures say He was to be born in Bethlehem. Do you want to know anything else?"

"No," said Herod, thinking. "That's enough."

So Herod sent everyone home. Then he met with the wise men in **secret.**

"The child," he whispered, "was born in Bethlehem. Go there, and tell me exactly where He is. I want to worship Him too. I do!"

Then Herod laughed to himself. *Camel brains!* he thought. *When I find that baby, I'll take care of Him. And I don't mean I'll change His diaper!*

The wise men traveled to Bethlehem. "Please, come in,"
said Mary when she discovered them at her door.

"The star led us here," they explained.

Jesus *peeked* around Mary's dress.

"Is this the King of the Jews?" they asked.

"Yes," said Mary, as Jesus toddled toward His visitors.

Jesus smiled at the wise men, and they bowed before Him.
"We have brought gifts for You," they said.

They unwrapped gold, frankincense, and myrrh.

The wise men slept peacefully that night. In their dreams, God warned them not to go back to Herod.

The wise men, in their WISDOM, obeyed. They agreed to travel back to their homeland without telling the wicked Herod anything at all.

Soon Herod learned that the wise men had tricked him. "Well, if they won't tell me which little boy is king, I'll get rid of *all* the baby boys!"

That night, an angel warned Joseph in a dream to escape to Egypt. Joseph and his little family obeyed. Then they waited in Egypt for the angel's return.

When it was safe, an angel again **appeared** to Joseph in a dream. He told Joseph to take Mary and the Son of God to Nazareth.

And so the prophecies—"I called my Son out of Egypt" and "He will be called a Nazarene"—came true.

God has given us the best gift of all—Jesus! His love keeps us **STRoNG** and helps us be good to others.

We can read all about Jesus in the Bible. That's why I'm giving one to Henrietta. I know that God wants her to know Jesus. He wants you to know Him too.

6 ONE LITTLE LUNCHBOX

Ugh! This fish smells like it's 2,000 years old! I'd better clean up this mess before my guests arrive.

What was I thinking? I invited all of my friends to a big dinner party. And then I told them to bring all of *their* friends. It'll take a MIRACLE to feed everyone—which reminds me of another hungry group back in Jesus' day.

Everywhere Jesus went, people followed. *Everywhere*. When Jesus walked, the people walked. When He sat, they sat. When He tried to take a nap, they hovered around Him.

Jesus attracted people like a light in the darkness attracts moths. They gathered in huge **CROWDS** just to hear His teachings. So He taught about God and performed miracles, like healing the sick.

Late one day, after healing a number of people, Jesus rowed across the Sea of Galilee. He wanted to rest with His followers. But before long, another large crowd had gathered.

Philip, one of Jesus' disciples, said, "This is crazy. Don't these people have homes? Don't they ever eat or sleep?"

Andrew yawned. "I don't know about them, but a **snooze** sounds good to me. Actually, so does an anchovy pizza!"

Luke, another follower, said, "Take note—these people will soon need nutritional supplementation."

Philip scratched his head. "Huh?"

"He means they're just as hungry as we are," Andrew explained.

"Good!" Philip said. "Let's send them home. Then we can order takeout."

Jesus sat down next to Philip. "These people have been here all day," He said. "Where can we buy some bread for them to eat?"

"**WHAT!?**" sputtered Philip. "There must be five thousand people here! Even if we all emptied our piggybanks, we could barely afford to feed each person a teensy cracker. Of course, we probably won't find a store open this late."

"Hmmm. I wonder if anyone brought snacks," Andrew mused. "Let's ask!"

Andrew and a few other disciples wandered through the crowd asking if anyone had food they could share.

But no one, it seemed, had brought any goodies. Discouraged, Andrew plopped down near a tree.

"Hey, mister!" a boy called down. "My mom packed me five loaves of barley bread and two LITTLE salted fish. You can have those!"

"Thank you!" Andrew said. But he thought: *I'll need at least a thousand lunchboxes to feed this bunch!*

Only Andrew came back from the crowd carrying food.

When Philip peered into the tiny lunchbox, he shook his head. "This will never be enough," he grumbled.

"What if we ground the bread and fish into a powder and put a pinch of it into everybody's water bottle?" Andrew suggested. "We could call it 'liquid vitamins'!"

Peter snorted. "These folks would get more vitamins chewing on their sandals."

Jesus chuckled. "Andrew, hand Me the lunchbox, please." Then He said to His disciples, "Tell everyone to sit down on the grass." When it got quiet, Jesus prayed, "Thank You, Father, for this barley bread and for these fish." Then He began to serve the bread and fish from the little lunchbox. The food just kept coming!

The people ate until their bellies **BULGED.** Then Jesus told His followers to gather up the leftovers. And they collected twelve big basketfuls. "Wow!" they exclaimed. "It's a miracle!"

No one went home hungry that day! I just hope my guests won't go home hungry today.

Look! Here they come. And it looks like they've brought enough food to feed Gideon's army!

Just as it says in Philippians 4:19, God has given me **EVERYTHiNG** I need—and then some!

Jesus Walks on Water

DARK & STORMY NIGHT

Whew! I've just finished staking my tomatoes. And look at my peppers, onions, and lettuce—*yuuummy!* Whenever I look at my garden, I can't help but give thanks to God for His miracle of creation. The dictionary says a *miracle* is something that can't be explained by science. I know that miracles always involve God.

Let's take a look at one of the many miracles Jesus performed with God's help. Believe me, this was something His followers never dreamed would happen!

Late one afternoon, Jesus wanted some quiet time with God. He told His followers to go ahead and take a **CRUISE** without Him.

"Come with us, Jesus," said the disciple who loved to captain the boat. "We'll ride some waves, catch some fish."

"No thanks. I need to go and pray," answered Jesus.

"Jesus sure likes to chat with God!" said Peter, another disciple.

As the disciples sailed away, Jesus began to pray.

Suddenly, fierce winds began to blow. *Whoosh. Whoosh.* And rain began to beat down. *Splash. Splash.*

"Ahoy!" cried the captain. "I can't **control** this thing. Batten down the hatches!"

"What hatches? We don't have any hatches," yelled a disciple.

"Then save yourselves!" the captain shouted. "Women and children first!"

"Hello?! There are no women or children," another voice grunted as they rowed for their lives.

Just before dawn, the disciples spotted something moving toward them across the water.

"Whoa! What's that?" cried the captain.

"A pogo stick?" guessed one follower.

"A really tall fish?" suggested another.

"Yikes! It's a GHOST!"

"Aaahh!" the others yelled in fright.

"Don't be afraid," they heard a voice say. "It's Me, Jesus."
Peter wasn't sure. "Lord, is that really You?" he asked.

"No worries," Jesus answered. "It's really Me."

"If You say so," Peter said, not quite convinced. "But if
it's **really** You, Lord, then tell me to walk over the water
to You."

"Come on," said Jesus.

Peter climbed over the boat's side. To his delight, he didn't plunge toward the bottom!

"Hey, look!" shouted Peter. "I can walk on water!"

Then Peter felt the wind whipping across his back. His **fear** returned, and he started to sink like a stone.

"Ack!" cried Peter. "Lord, save me!"

The other disciples watched helplessly from the boat.

But Jesus grabbed Peter's hand and pulled him back to the surface.

"Peter, why did you **DOUBT?**" asked Jesus. "What happened to your faith?"

"Maybe I dropped it in the water?" Peter replied sheepishly. Then he added, "Nah, I just got scared and lost it. I'm sorry."

As Jesus and Peter clambered into the boat, the winds slowed and the waves calmed.

"Awesome, Lord! You saved Peter," said the captain.

"It's a miracle!" shouted another disciple. "There's only one explanation. You really *are* the **Son of God!**"

Everyone in the boat agreed. And they all worshiped Jesus.

The miracles Jesus performed helped people to see that He is the Son of God. Today, God's miracles—like Creation—open new eyes every day. Think about it. Who but God could have dreamed up an aardvark or a kumquat or even you?!

John 1:3 says, "All things were made through [God]. Nothing was made without Him."

Remember that the next time you pluck a ripe tomato or look at yourself in the mirror. Thank God for His miracle of life. Especially the life you can have through Jesus Christ, His Son.

Jesus Raises the Dead
LAZARUS LIVES

Boy, does my tummy hurt! I must have eaten too much pizza. My grandma used to make hot tea for me whenever I got sick, and it always made me feel better. That's why I'm making some now.

Hmm, I wonder if tea would have helped Lazarus feel better? Probably not; he was really, *really* sick. He needed special help from Jesus to get well.

One day Lazarus complained to his sisters. "Mary! Martha! I feel awful. My head hurts. My stomach hurts. Even my beard hurts."

"I'll fix you some tea," said Martha.

But when she offered it to him, Lazarus just groaned.

"I'll ask our neighbor Bill to find Jesus," said Mary. "He'll know what to do."

Bill saddled his donkey and rode away. He found Jesus in a distant village.

"Your friend Lazarus is very sick," said Bill. "Please come quickly."

Jesus SMILED. "Don't worry, My friend," He answered. "Lazarus will be fine. You'll see."

A couple of days later, Jesus said to His disciples, "Let's take a trip to Judea and see Lazarus."

"But Jesus," said Peter, "the last time we were there, people tried to kill You!"

"Remember the servant of that Roman soldier?" asked John. "You **healed** him without ever seeing him. Why can't You heal Lazarus from here—where it's safe?!"

"I must go," Jesus answered. "Lazarus has fallen asleep, and I must wake him."

Mary and Martha sat by their brother's bed, **SOBBING.**
"I can't believe Lazarus is really gone," Mary cried.

"Neither can I," Martha said. Then she loudly blew her
nose. "But I guess we have to accept that our brother has
died. Mary, if you'll help the servants prepare his body, I'll
go and tell our friends."

Jesus finally reached Judea—four days after Lazarus had died.

When Martha heard He was in town, she *ran* to meet Him.

"Lord," she said, "if You had been here, my brother wouldn't have died." Then she added in a softer voice, "But I know that even now God will give You anything You ask."

Jesus stood very still. "Martha," He said. "I am the resurrection and the life. He who believes in Me will have 𝐿𝐼𝐹𝐸 even if he dies. And he who lives and believes in Me will never die. Do you believe this?"

"Oh yes!" Martha answered. "I do believe."

Jesus followed Martha back to her house. Tears filled His eyes when He saw how sad everyone was.

"Lead Me to the tomb," He said.

Jesus ordered that the tomb be opened, but Martha said, "Um . . . Lazarus has been in there for four days. He'll be stinky!"

"Do you believe or don't you?" Jesus asked.

"I believe," said Martha. And the tomb was **OPENED.**

Jesus prayed in a loud voice, "Father, thank You for hearing Me. I know You always hear Me. But I speak loudly now so the people around Me may hear and believe You sent Me."

Then Jesus called, "Lazarus come out!"

Lazarus obeyed, still wrapped in his burial cloths. Amazing!

Wow! I feel much better now. Just like I did when Grandma made me tea and told me Bible stories. By George, that's it! There's just something about Bible stories that makes me feel good!

Mary and Martha must have felt even **BETTER** than good when Lazarus walked out of his tomb. They knew it was a miracle.

Jesus has given us the miracle of eternal life with Him— He only asks that we, like Martha, believe.

The Good Samaritan
DOING UNTO OTHERS

Ouchie, Mama! I think I've sprained my ankle. I should have fixed that loose board a long time ago.

Good thing I left my old medical bag where I can reach it. Let's see what I've got—Band-Aids, smelly goop . . . and lollipops! Looks like I can take care of my **boo-boo** until someone comes along to help me up.

I feel a little like the traveler from Jesus' story about a very helpful man . . .

One day, a teacher asked Jesus lots of questions about how to get into heaven. Jesus responded by asking the teacher what the law books said.

"Love the Lord God with all your heart, all your soul, all your strength, and all your mind," the teacher answered. "And it says, 'love your neighbor as you love yourself.'"

"Well, there's your answer," Jesus commented.

"Wait," the teacher said. "I still don't get it. Who counts as my neighbor?"

To explain, Jesus told the teacher the story of the Good
Samaritan.

A man once traveled down the road to Jericho. Enjoying his
outing, he whistled a happy tune as he walked. This traveler
didn't notice two sneaky **ROBBERS** hiding in the bushes.

The robbers jumped into the road and tackled the traveler.
Then they beat him up and ran away, leaving him on the side
of the road.

A short while later, a priest zipped by. *I must get to temple,* thought the **priest.** *Mounds of work to do . . . Temple bazaar to plan . . . Sermon to compose . . .*

But when he heard a long moan—"Ohhh-aagh"—he screeched to a stop. Then he saw the injured traveler.

Hmmm. That man sounds hurt. Wish I had time to help him. Maybe he won't notice me if I'm on the other side of the road.

The priest crossed the road and jogged away, covering his face. But God still saw him.

Soon, another worker from the temple scooted down the road.

As he walked, he prayed, "Oh, my dear Lord, my precious Lord, I want to be Your servant. Oh, I'm Yours, I'm Yours, I'm Yours. Yes, I want to help people and do good."

He *tripped* over the hurt traveler.

"Who left this man in the middle of the road? How rude . . . anyway, as I was saying, Lord, use me to help others."

And he continued down the road.

Before long, someone else came by.

"Whoa, Gertrude. Slow down," said the man from Samaria to his donkey. He had spotted the hurt traveler.

"May I help you, partner?" asked the Good **Samaritan.** The traveler moaned and tried to whistle his happy tune.

Good Sammy grabbed his medical bag, cleaned the traveler's wounds, and put Band-Aids on them. Then he helped the traveler climb onto Gertrude, and they headed for town.

The Good Samaritan took the traveler to a five-star hotel with room service, fluffy pillows, and nice cotton sheets.

Good Sammy said to the innkeeper, "Here's **MONEY** for the traveler's room. And here's a little extra, in case he needs some curly fries or an ice cream. Take good care of him. If he needs anything else, I'll pay for it when I return."

"So someone finally helped the traveler," finished Jesus. Then He asked, "Now which of those three—the priest, the righteous man, or the Samaritan—acted as a good **neighbor?**"

"Good Sammy, of course!" answered the teacher. "He stopped and helped. He was giving and loving and all that good stuff."

"That's right," said Jesus. "He loved another as he loved himself. Now, go out and try to love your neighbor just like the Samaritan did."

We must help others when we see their needs. We can't assume someone else will come along.

Slow down and make time to **HeLP,** even if you're in a hurry. God has given us each precious gifts. Don't take them for granted. Instead, use them to help others.

I think I'll take a little nap until my own good neighbor comes to lend *me* a hand!

SERVING THE DESERVING

Tagalong and I walked nearly two miles before that downpour hit. Jogging home in the rain sure refreshes the soul—and muddies the feet.

Ew! Look at this! My feet are filthy! I could start a vegetable garden here!

I'd better put this towel to good use if I want to keep the kitchen floor clean.

This towel reminds me of a story that took place in Jesus' day.

In Bible times, people walked just about everywhere. And they wore sandals, which meant their little piggies got pretty dirty. This little piggy stomped in puddles. This little piggy splashed in mud. And this little piggy squished into a camel pie! Gross!

No wonder people handed visitors a basin of water and a towel to clean their tootsies at the door. Often a servant SCRUB-A-DUB-DUBBED guests' feet before they came inside.

One day, the disciples headed to a dinner party at Jesus' house. "Come on, you slowpokes," Peter said to the other disciples.

Peter jogged ahead. "Jesus has something important to tell us," he called over his shoulder, "and I don't want to miss it."

"Peter! Really!" John replied. "If it's that important, Jesus will wait until we get there to say it."

Then Peter spied the house where Jesus was staying. "Hey! Last one there does the **dishes,**" he yelled, breaking into a full run.

Jesus opened the door. "Wow! You're early!" He said. "Please come in and sit down."

"But our feet are dirty," Peter pointed out.

"Never mind about that now," Jesus replied. "Just come in."

The disciples sat around a **BANQUET** table heaped with fruit salad, lamb burgers, and goat milkshakes—the works! Mmmm.

The disciples chatted about the hottest new oxcarts while they ate. Then, saying He'd be right back, Jesus left the room.

The water in the basin sloshed as Jesus carried it into the room. He had wrapped a clean towel around His waist.

"John!" said Jesus. "Scoot around in your chair so I can wash your feet."

"Well, um, okay—w-whatever You say," John stammered.

Once John's feet were clean, Jesus turned to James. "You're next," Jesus said.

Splash! Scrub! Pat-pat-pat! James wiggled his spotless toes.

"Peter?" Jesus said. "Your feet, please!"

"What? No way! I—You—we—that is—" Peter sputtered.

Jesus smiled. "It's okay, Peter. You don't understand now, but you will later. May I have your feet?"

Peter pounded the table with his fist. **"NO!"** he thundered. "You will never wash my feet. You are our King, not our servant."

"If I don't wash your feet, then you are not one of My people," said Jesus.

Peter shoved himself away from the table. "Then give me a **whole** bath!" he cried.

Jesus smiled. "Just a foot bath will do," He said.

Peter stuck out his feet. "Sorry about that camel pie," he muttered. "We were racing and . . . well . . ."

After Jesus had washed everyone's feet, He said, "Today I became your SERVANT. Every good leader must serve others—showing kindness to everyone, regardless of who they are." He looked at Peter and grinned. "Or what they have on their feet."

Then Jesus told His disciples, "Follow My example. Be thoughtful and kind to everyone."

Jesus wants us to love others just like we love ourselves. And serving others shows them we love them—just like Jesus loved His disciples, and like He **L♥VES** us.

Well, my feet are clean! And to show Tagalong how much I love her, I'll wash hers next. Hey! Tagalong, where are you going? Come back, girl! Come here and let me wash your feet!

JUST THE WAY YOU ARE

I've been looking for a **new** pair of sandals. But these hardly look new. They've got holes so big that my toes are leaking out. Whoever walked around in these babies probably wore out their feet too.

Jesus walked all the time—just to help people. His sandals probably looked something like these.

One day, Jesus and His buddies hiked through Judea. They taught the people there to spread the Good News about God.

Everyone seemed to get into the spirit of things. Well, everyone except a grumpy guy named MELVIN. He didn't like crowds.

"Oh," moaned Melvin, "swarms of people are rushing this way. Come on, Jesus. Let's sneak down another path."

"There He is!" a mom yelled, toting her two children.

As the mob rushed over, the grumpy guy threw himself between Jesus and the crowd, shouting, "Go away."

But the determined parents ignored him, pleading: "Jesus, please bless my child." "Jesus, can You heal my son's wart?" "Lord, please fix my daughter's voice. She can't sing a note."

Melvin shouted, "Get back! Take every wart, every vocal cord, every wet little face home! Jesus is too busy for your germy rug rats."

Calmly, Jesus said, "Let all the kids come to Me."
Jesus opened His arms and hugged all the children.

"Hello, Rachael," Jesus said. He brushed His hand across
her little head. "Good to see you, Hannah and Roberto."

Something tickled Jesus' toes. Was it a bug? He looked
down and discovered a little girl playing with His sandals.

"Would you like to try on My sandals, Ruthie?"

The child BEAMED as she pulled on sandals
that were way too big.

"Jesus, shouldn't we be doing something more important?" asked the grumpy guy. "Don't we have hungry people to heal and sick people to feed . . . or something like that?"

"My dear Melvin," said Jesus kindly, "I also love to spend time with little **children,** like these."

Jesus gathered everyone around and spoke softly, as if He were sharing a big secret.

"God's kingdom belongs to children like these. No one can go to heaven without becoming like children."

The grumpy guy's eyes filled with tears, and his lower lip began to droop and wiggle.

"I-I can't go to heaven if I'm not a little boy?" Melvin whined.

"That's not what I meant," answered Jesus.

"Children have the qualities God loves most," Jesus explained. "They trust Him. They are open with their feelings. They have faith in others. In these ways, we should never stop being like children. And we should always stop to help children in need."

Grumpy guy wiped away a tear.

"I'm sorry for keeping these little ones away," he said. "Even though they have wet faces."

Jesus smiled. "Your face is pretty wet too, buddy." And Melvin's grumpiness slipped away.

Clasping hands, everyone formed a CIRCLE around Jesus and Melvin and began to sing:

Jesus loves the little children,
All the children of the world.
Any color, dark or light,
They are precious in his sight.
Jesus loves the little children of the world.
— Adapted by Mrs. Dan Whitaker

Melvin learned one of the best lessons that day. He learned how important it is to help all people! No matter what they look like, where they live, or how young they are.

Jesus loves everyone! And we should too.

So take a good look at the people around you, and do something right **NOW** to help someone else. A good deed shows how much we care and reminds people how much Jesus loves us all!

GOD SO LOVED THE WORLD

The Bible is a letter of love from God to you and me. No, not a *gushy* love letter with hearts and kisses, but a "letter" of love.

In it, God tells us how much He wants us to live with Him forever in heaven. But to do that, we have to be perfect—without sin. Are you perfect? I know I'm not. So how are we supposed to get to heaven?

To find out, you have to read God's first letter, which starts . . .

In the beginning, God created Adam and Eve. They lived in the perfect Garden of Eden.

God told them, "Eat anything you want—except the fruit from the tree of the knowledge of good and evil."

They obeyed **UNTiL** a sneaky snake convinced Eve to disobey God and taste the tree's forbidden fruit. Adam ate some too.

Oops! Big problem. When A&E disobeyed God, sin entered the world. Adam and Eve had to leave Eden. And because of *their* sin, everyone else was born sinful—even you and me!

But God had a plan—long before He created the world. A plan to $\mathcal{SAVE}$ us!

God's perfect plan came to earth when His Son, Jesus, was born in Bethlehem. God chose Mary to be Jesus' mother and Joseph to be His earthly father.

The angels announced Jesus' birth. Shepherds and wise men received the news with joy. At last! A Savior had come.

Jesus became a teacher. His disciples learned about God's love. Jesus taught them to show God's L♥VE through serving and helping others. Once, Jesus showed what He meant by washing His disciples' feet—this was something only a servant would do.

Jesus also explained that He came to earth to save people from their sins. Several times, He said, "I will be killed. But I will come back again."

His disciples didn't like to hear that.

But Jesus taught the importance of trust and faith. Peter found out what Jesus meant when he and some other disciples saw Jesus walk on top of a **stormy** lake. Peter wanted to walk on the water too.

He stepped out of the boat and trusted Jesus. Peter's faith was so strong that he was able to take a few steps on top of the water. But he suddenly lost his courage. He saw the big waves and became afraid. Down, down, down, Peter sank.

But Jesus was right there to save Peter.

Jesus performed other miracles too. He healed people, and one time, He even brought His friend Lazarus back to LIFE. Another time, Jesus fed more than 5,000 people with just five loaves of barley bread and two dried fish.

The crowd thought that was amazing. It was a true miracle!

While many people loved Jesus, others were jealous of Him and hated Him. Still others *wanted* Jesus to be the king of Israel.

When Jesus talked about His Kingdom, people thought He meant He would destroy the cruel Roman Empire. Even His disciples didn't understand that Jesus had come to destroy something even worse—sin!

Did the fact that Jesus had enemies surprise God? Nope! Nothing surprises God.

God knew Judas, one of Jesus' closest friends, would betray His Son. God heard the people lie about Jesus. And He heard the words, "Crucify Him!" He could have stopped it, but He didn't.

Jesus allowed Himself to be nailed to a cross and die because that was part of God's plan. But that wasn't the *whole* plan.

Three days later, the most wonderful thing happened. Jesus came back to life again. He **defeated** sin!

God's letter of love tells us that Jesus died on the cross so that our sins could be forgiven. If we ask Jesus to forgive us of our sins and live in our hearts, He will. What a gift!

God loves you so much. He gives you a guide to make you more like Him. That's right: The Bible—God's love letter to you. Learn to stay in His "letter" of love, and you will get to know your best friend, Jesus, better and better.

BYE NOW!